Mastering Social Media

Unlock the Secrets to Grow, Engage, and Succeed Online

CONSULTORIA IA

Mastering Social Media

Unlock the Secrets to Grow, Engage, and Succeed Online

CONSULTORIA IA

CONSULTORIA IA

Mastering Social Media

Unlock the Secrets to Grow, Engage, and Succeed Online

Copyright © 2024 by Consultoria IA

All rights reserved. No part of this publication may be reproduced, stored or transmitted in any form or by any means, electronic, mechanical, photocopying, recording, scanning, or otherwise without written permission from the publisher. It is illegal to copy this book, post it to a website, or distribute it by any other means without permission.

First edition

This book was professionally typeset on Reedsy
Find out more at reedsy.com

Contents

Mastering Social Media: Unlock the Secrets to Grow, Engage, and Succeed Online

Review

Why Read "Mastering Social Media: Unlock the Secrets to Grow, Engage, and Succeed Online"?

Target Audience

Preface

Chapter 1: The Foundations of Social Media Success

Chapter 2: Creating Content That Captivates

Chapter 3: The Power of Analytics and Metrics

Chapter 4: Building Genuine Engagement and Community

Chapter 5: Monetizing Your Social Media Presence

Appendices

Mastering Social Media: Unlock the Secrets to Grow, Engage, and Succeed Online

Review

This book is an essential guide for anyone looking to harness the full potential of social media in today's digital world. Written with a practical and approachable style, **"Mastering Social Media"** breaks down key strategies to build a strong presence, attract engaged followers, and turn online interactions into real success.

With real-world examples and up-to-date advice, the book covers a variety of platforms, including Facebook, Instagram, LinkedIn, TikTok, and more. It also provides practical tools for analyzing metrics, creating impactful content, and managing advertising campaigns efficiently.

Whether you're an entrepreneur, a content creator, or a marketing professional, this eBook equips you with the skills needed to stand out in the competitive online landscape and achieve your goals with confidence.

Why Read "Mastering Social Media: Unlock the Secrets to Grow, Engage, and Succeed Online"?

In the fast-paced digital age, social media is no longer optional—it's essential. This book is your ultimate roadmap to navigating the ever-changing social media landscape with confidence and purpose. Here's why you should read it:

Actionable Strategies: Gain access to proven techniques that help you grow your audience, boost engagement, and achieve measurable results.

Platform-Specific Insights: Learn how to maximize your impact on key platforms like Facebook, Instagram, LinkedIn, TikTok, and more.

Content That Converts: Discover how to create content that not only grabs attention but also drives meaningful interactions and outcomes.

Stay Ahead of Trends: Get up-to-date guidance on emerging trends and tools, ensuring you stay ahead in the competitive social media space.

For All Levels: Whether you're a beginner or an experienced marketer, the book is packed with tips that are easy to understand and implement.

Achieve Your Goals: Whether you want to grow a personal brand, promote a business, or become a content creator, this book gives you the skills and confidence to succeed.

Invest in yourself and your online presence—this book is a must-read for anyone serious about thriving in today's connected world.

Target Audience

This book is designed to cater to a diverse group of readers who are eager to leverage social media to achieve their goals. The key target audiences include:

Entrepreneurs and Small Business Owners

Learn how to build a compelling online presence to attract customers, increase sales, and grow your brand without a massive marketing budget.

Content Creators and Influencers

Discover strategies for growing your audience, boosting engagement, and monetizing your content across various platforms.

Marketing Professionals

Stay updated on the latest trends and tools to drive successful campaigns and measure ROI effectively.

Students and Aspiring Professionals

Gain foundational knowledge and hands-on skills to kickstart a career in digital marketing or social media management.

Nonprofits and Community Leaders

Use social media to amplify your message, rally supporters, and create impactful campaigns for your cause.

Anyone New to Social Media

Get a step-by-step introduction to understanding and mastering the basics, ensuring you can navigate the digital landscape with confidence.

No matter your level of expertise or industry, this book provides the tools and insights you need to make social media work for you.

Preface

In today's world, social media isn't just a tool—it's a game changer. It has transformed how we communicate, connect, and do business. What began as a way to share photos and status updates has evolved into a dynamic ecosystem where brands are built, careers are launched, and communities are forged.

This book was born out of a simple realization: while the potential of social media is enormous, so is the confusion around how to truly master it. With constantly shifting algorithms, emerging platforms, and an overwhelming amount of advice online, it can feel impossible to know where to start or how to stand out.

Through *Mastering Social Media*, my goal is to cut through the noise and offer a clear, actionable roadmap to success. This isn't just about getting more likes or followers—it's about creating genuine connections, achieving your goals, and making a lasting impact.

Whether you're an entrepreneur looking to grow your business, a content creator striving to build a loyal audience, or someone simply wanting to navigate the digital space with confidence, this book is for you. It combines practical strategies, real-world examples, and the latest insights to ensure you're always one step ahead.

Social media is more than a platform—it's an opportunity. I hope this book inspires you to seize it, embrace your unique voice, and unlock your full potential online.

Let's dive in together.

CONSULTORIA IA

Chapter 1: The Foundations of Social Media Success

Welcome to the world of social media, where billions of people connect, share, and interact daily. Whether you're a budding influencer, a brand looking to grow, or an entrepreneur seeking to expand your reach, this chapter lays the groundwork for your success. Let's uncover the principles and strategies that separate those who thrive from those who merely survive.

1. Understanding the Power of Social Media

In 2023, over 4.9 billion people actively use social media—that's more than half the world's population. Platforms like Instagram, TikTok, LinkedIn, and Twitter have become more than social hubs; they're powerful tools for marketing, branding, and communication. But success doesn't come from merely being present. It requires understanding the unique dynamics of these platforms and how to align them with your goals.

Did you know? 90% of consumers say they'll buy from a brand they follow on social media. That's a staggering statistic that underscores the importance of cultivating a strong and authentic online presence.

2. Setting Clear Goals

Every successful social media strategy begins with clear, measurable objectives. Ask yourself:

Why am I using social media? Is it to build brand awareness, generate leads, drive traffic, or establish authority?

Who is my target audience? Understanding your audience's demographics, interests, and online behavior is critical.

What does success look like? Define KPIs (Key Performance Indicators) such as follower growth, engagement rates, or conversions.

Pro Tip: Set SMART goals (Specific, Measurable, Achievable, Relevant, Time-bound). For example, "Increase Instagram engagement by 20% within three months" is far more effective than a vague "Get more likes."

3. Choosing the Right Platforms

Not all social media platforms are created equal, nor are they suited to every goal. Focus on the platforms where your target audience is most active.

Instagram and TikTok: Great for visually-driven content and younger audiences.

LinkedIn: Ideal for B2B connections, thought leadership, and professional networking.

Facebook: Still a strong choice for community-building and targeted ads.

Twitter: Perfect for real-time updates and engaging in trending conversations.

Insider Insight: Studies show that brands active on 2-3 platforms perform better than those spreading themselves too thin. Depth trumps breadth when it comes to content creation and audience engagement.

4. Crafting Your Unique Brand Voice

Your social media presence should reflect a consistent and compelling brand identity. This goes beyond logos and color schemes; it's about how you communicate and connect.

Be Authentic: People value transparency. Share stories, challenges, and successes that resonate with your audience.

Stay Consistent: Whether it's a witty, professional, or inspirational tone, consistency builds trust and recognition.

Engage Actively: Social media is a two-way street. Reply to comments, ask questions, and participate in discussions.

Real-Life Example: Look at Wendy's on Twitter. Their playful, cheeky tone has turned the brand into a social media phenomenon with millions of engaged followers.

5. Mastering Content Strategy

The saying "Content is king" holds true, but not all content is created equal. A strong content strategy ensures you deliver value while aligning with your goals.

Content Pillars: Define 3-5 core themes (e.g., education, entertainment, behind-the-scenes) that resonate with your audience.

Quality Over Quantity: Posting frequently is important, but quality content that sparks engagement is key.

Experiment and Evolve: Monitor what works through analytics and adjust your strategy as needed.

Action Step: Plan a content calendar to stay consistent. Tools like Hootsuite, Buffer, or even a simple spreadsheet can help you organize your posts.

6. Leveraging Analytics and Insights

Data is your best friend in social media success. Regularly analyze your performance to understand what's working and where to improve.

Engagement Metrics: Likes, comments, shares, and saves.

Reach and Impressions: How many people saw your content.

Conversion Rates: Actions taken, such as clicks, sign-ups, or purchases.

Stat to Ponder: Posts with video content receive 48% more views than those without. Consider incorporating more videos into your strategy.

7. Staying Agile and Adapting

Social media trends evolve rapidly. What worked six months ago might not work today. Staying flexible and experimenting with new formats (like Reels, Stories, or carousels) can give you an edge.

Monitor Trends: Follow industry leaders and trending hashtags to stay ahead.

Test and Learn: A/B test different approaches, such as varying captions or experimenting with posting times.

Key Takeaway: Your willingness to adapt separates you from competitors who remain stagnant.

The foundations of social media success lie in understanding your audience, setting clear goals, and consistently delivering valuable content. But beyond strategy, success requires patience, persistence, and a genuine desire to connect. Remember, social media isn't just about numbers—it's about building relationships and creating a meaningful impact.

Are you ready to embark on this journey? Let's dive deeper in the next chapters to uncover advanced strategies and tools to elevate your social media game.

Understanding the Core Principles of Building an Effective Social Media Presence

In today's interconnected world, a robust social media presence is not just an asset—it's a necessity. Whether you're a small business owner, a budding influencer, or part of a large corporation, social media serves as the bridge to connect with your audience, amplify your brand, and drive measurable growth. But here's the kicker: many dive headfirst into the social media pool without a strategy, only to find themselves floundering. To succeed, you need to start with the basics—the core principles that form the foundation of an effective social media strategy. Let's break it down together, step by step.

Principle #1: Define Your Goals

Before you post a single tweet or share your first Instagram story, you need clarity. What are you trying to achieve? Without a goal, your efforts will lack direction and measurable success. According to a 2023 HubSpot survey, 83% of marketers who set specific goals for their social media campaigns report higher success rates than those who don't.

Ask Yourself:

Are you trying to increase brand awareness?

Generate leads or drive sales?

Foster community engagement?

Provide stellar customer service?

Each goal requires a different approach. For instance, if your focus is brand awareness, your metrics of success may include impressions and reach. However, if sales are your goal, track conversions and ROI instead. Write your goals down—they're your North Star.

Principle #2: Understand Your Target Audience

If your content is for everyone, it's for no one. A scattergun approach dilutes your message and misses the opportunity to truly connect with those who matter. Instead, craft a vivid picture of your ideal audience. Who are they? What are their pain points, and where do they hang out online?

Practical Steps to Define Your Audience:

Conduct Surveys: Directly ask existing customers about their preferences and behaviors.

Use Analytics Tools: Platforms like Facebook Insights, Twitter Analytics, and Google Analytics reveal demographic and psychographic details.

Create Buyer Personas: These fictional profiles of your ideal customers should include details like age, gender, location, interests, and challenges.

Pro Tip: Did you know 74% of consumers expect brands to understand their needs and expectations? (Source: Salesforce, 2023). When you speak directly to your audience, engagement soars.

Principle #3: Choose the Right Platforms

There are dozens of social media platforms, but you don't need to be everywhere. Focus your energy where your target audience spends their time.

Platform Highlights:

Instagram: Best for visual storytelling and younger demographics.

LinkedIn: Ideal for B2B marketing and professional networking.

TikTok: A goldmine for creative, short-form content targeting Gen Z and millennials.

Facebook: Great for community building and reaching older demographics.

Twitter/X: Perfect for news updates and real-time engagement.

Actionable Insight: According to DataReportal, as of 2024, Instagram boasts over 2.35 billion active users, while TikTok's engagement rates are 6x higher than Instagram's. These platforms are not just options—they're opportunities. Choose wisely.

Principle #4: Create Value-Driven Content

Content is king, but not just any content. Your audience craves content that informs, entertains, or solves a problem.

Content Ideas That Deliver:

Educational Posts: Share how-to guides, tips, and actionable insights. For example, a fitness coach might post "10-Minute Workouts for Busy Professionals."

Engaging Stories: Humans love stories—it's in our DNA. Share behind-the-scenes glimpses or client success stories.

Interactive Formats: Polls, quizzes, and Q&A sessions invite audience participation and build engagement.

Stats That Speak Volumes:

Visual content is 40x more likely to get shared on social media (Buffer, 2023).

Posts with videos get 48% more views than static posts (Sprout Social, 2023).

When creating content, focus on your audience's needs. What questions are they asking? What's keeping them up at night? Answer those questions through your posts.

Principle #5: Consistency is Key

Social media success doesn't happen overnight. It's a marathon, not a sprint. Consistency in posting builds trust and keeps your brand top-of-mind.

Tips for Staying Consistent:

Use a content calendar to schedule posts in advance.

Post at optimal times based on platform analytics.

Maintain a cohesive brand voice and aesthetic.

Did You Know? Brands that post consistently are 76% more likely to see engagement growth within six months (Hootsuite, 2023).

Principle #6: Engage, Don't Just Broadcast

Social media is a two-way street. If all you're doing is posting without engaging, you're missing half the equation. Responding to comments, answering DMs, and actively participating in conversations foster a sense of community.

Engagement Tips:

Reply to comments within 24 hours.

Use the platform's tools, such as polls and questions, to invite dialogue.

Collaborate with influencers and brand advocates to reach wider audiences.

Engagement isn't just about keeping current followers happy—it's about amplifying your reach. Posts with high engagement are favored by algorithms, increasing visibility.

Principle #7: Measure and Optimize

You can't improve what you don't measure. Regularly review your analytics to see what's working and what isn't.

Key Metrics to Track:

Engagement Rate: Likes, comments, shares, and clicks divided by impressions.

Reach and Impressions: How many people saw your post?

Conversion Rate: The percentage of users who took a desired action (e.g., signing up for a newsletter).

Tools like Hootsuite, Buffer, and Sprout Social offer detailed insights into your social performance. Use this data to tweak your strategy. Maybe your audience prefers reels over static posts, or perhaps LinkedIn outperforms Twitter for B2B leads. Adapt and evolve.

Building an effective social media presence isn't about ticking off a checklist. It's a dynamic process that requires experimentation, adaptation, and persistence. Remember, every brand's journey is unique, and there's no one-size-fits-all strategy.

Dear reader, what's your next move? Will you revisit your goals or dive deeper into audience research? Whatever it is, take the first step today. Social media waits for no one—and your competitors certainly won't.

Now it's over to you. What's the most valuable insight you gained from this guide? Leave a comment and let's keep the conversation going. The world of social media is vast, but together, we can navigate it and thrive.

Chapter 2: Creating Content That Captivates

In the ever-changing world of social media, content is king. It's the heartbeat of every successful social media strategy and the magnet that attracts and retains your audience. This chapter delves into how you can create content that not only grabs attention but also sparks meaningful engagement and loyalty. By the end, you'll have a roadmap to crafting captivating content that resonates with your target audience, drives action, and builds a thriving online community.

The Power of Storytelling

Human beings are hardwired for stories. A well-told story can evoke emotions, inspire action, and create a memorable connection between you and your audience. In the digital realm, storytelling isn't just about words—it encompasses images, videos, and even user interactions.

Key Elements of a Great Story:

Relatable Characters: Showcase real people, relatable personas, or aspirational figures to make your content feel authentic.

Conflict and Resolution: Every story thrives on tension. Identify a problem your audience faces and show how it's resolved, with your brand or message as the hero.

Emotion: People remember how you make them feel. Use humor, inspiration, nostalgia, or empathy to leave a lasting impression.

Action Tip:

Use Instagram Stories, TikTok, or YouTube to share a behind-the-scenes look at your brand. Let your audience see the human side of your business, struggles, and victories—and invite them to be part of the journey.

Understanding Your Audience

Captivating content starts with a deep understanding of your audience. Who are they? What are their pain points, desires, and values? Understanding your audience allows you to craft messages that resonate and speak directly to them.

Steps to Understand Your Audience:

Analyze Demographics: Use platform insights (e.g., Facebook Insights, Instagram Analytics) to understand age, gender, location, and more.

Engage with Your Community: Conduct polls, surveys, or Q&A sessions to hear directly from your followers.

Monitor Trends: Stay updated on trending topics and hashtags that matter to your audience.

Create Personas: Develop detailed personas of your ideal followers, including their challenges, goals, and preferred content styles.

Action Tip:

Build a persona of your ideal audience member. For example:

Name: Sarah

Age: 28

Interests: Fitness, healthy eating, personal growth

Social Media Preference: Instagram and Pinterest

Content Preference: Quick tips, inspiring stories, and vibrant visuals

Design your content as if you were speaking directly to Sarah.

The Anatomy of Captivating Content

What makes a piece of content scroll-stopping and irresistible? The answer lies in a combination of creativity, strategy, and a deep understanding of your audience. Let's break it down:

1. Visual Appeal

Your audience's first impression often comes from your visuals. High-quality, eye-catching images and videos are essential for captivating content.

Use Vibrant Colors: Bright, bold colors tend to grab attention in crowded feeds.

Consistency Matters: Maintain a consistent visual style (filters, fonts, and layouts) to reinforce brand recognition.

Leverage Video: Short-form videos (15-60 seconds) perform exceptionally well on platforms like Instagram Reels and TikTok.

Action Tip:

Use tools like Canva or Adobe Express to design professional graphics, or experiment with editing apps like CapCut for videos.

2. Headlines and Captions That Spark Interest

Your headline or caption is the gateway to your content. A strong, intriguing headline can dramatically improve engagement.

Ask Questions: "What's the best piece of advice you've ever received?"
Create a Sense of Urgency: "Don't miss this limited-time offer!"
Use Numbers: "5 Simple Steps to Grow Your Instagram"

Action Tip:

A/B test your captions to see what style resonates most with your audience.

3. Interactive Elements

Interactive content transforms passive scrolling into active participation. It's also an excellent way to gather feedback and insights.

Polls and Quizzes: Ask your audience their opinion on relevant topics.

Contests and Giveaways: Encourage users to tag friends, share posts, or create user-generated content.

Live Streams: Host Q&A sessions, tutorials, or product launches in real-time.

Action Tip:

Host a weekly Instagram Live where you answer follower questions. Promote it beforehand to build anticipation.

4. Value-Driven Content

Ensure your content serves a purpose: educating, entertaining, inspiring, or solving a problem.

Educational Posts: Share tutorials, tips, or how-tos.

Entertaining Content: Use humor, memes, or relatable scenarios to make your audience laugh.

Inspirational Stories: Share quotes, testimonials, or uplifting anecdotes.

Action Tip:

Create a content calendar with a mix of these types to ensure variety and consistent value.

Leveraging Data to Optimize Content

Data-driven insights are invaluable for refining your content strategy. Analytics help you understand what works and what doesn't, allowing you to focus your efforts effectively.

Metrics to Monitor:

Engagement Rate: Likes, comments, shares, and saves indicate how well your content resonates.

Reach and Impressions: Measure how many people saw your content and how often.

Click-Through Rate (CTR): For links, track how many users clicked.

Conversion Rate: Evaluate how many users completed a desired action (e.g., signing up for a newsletter).

Action Tip:

Use tools like Google Analytics, Hootsuite, or native platform insights to track your performance. Identify patterns in your top-performing posts and replicate their success.

Adapting Content for Different Platforms

Each social media platform has its unique culture and audience preferences. What works on one platform might not resonate on another.

Instagram:

Visual-first: Prioritize high-quality images and short-form videos.

Stories: Use this feature for casual, behind-the-scenes content.

TikTok:

Trendy and Fun: Leverage challenges, popular sounds, and quirky content.

Authenticity Rules: Raw, unfiltered content often performs better than polished productions.

LinkedIn:

Professional Tone: Share industry insights, thought leadership, and professional milestones.

Long-Form Posts: Articles or detailed posts perform well.

Twitter:

Concise and Witty: Stick to the character limit with snappy, engaging tweets.

Real-Time Engagement: Participate in trending topics and hashtags.

Action Tip:

Repurpose content creatively. For instance, turn a long-form blog into a Twitter thread, an Instagram carousel, and a TikTok video.

Case Studies: Brands That Captivate

1. Nike

Nike's social media campaigns excel by blending powerful storytelling with visually compelling content. Their "You Can't Stop Us" campaign resonated globally by showcasing diverse athletes overcoming challenges.

Lesson:

Use emotionally charged stories and align them with your brand values to inspire and connect with your audience.

2. Glossier

Glossier thrives by encouraging user-generated content and leveraging it to showcase authentic customer experiences.

Lesson:

Empower your audience to share their stories and celebrate their contributions to your brand.

3. Duolingo

Duolingo's playful and meme-centric TikTok strategy has helped the brand connect with a younger audience in an authentic way.

Lesson:

Don't be afraid to embrace humor and trends to humanize your brand.

Practical Exercises to Master Content Creation

The 10-10-10 Rule:

Spend 10 minutes brainstorming content ideas.

Spend 10 minutes creating one piece of content.

Spend 10 minutes reviewing and improving it.

Content Audit:

Review your last 20 posts.

Identify patterns in high-performing content and note what can be improved.

Creative Challenge:

Choose a trending topic or hashtag.

Create three different types of posts (e.g., a meme, a short video, and an infographic).

Creating captivating content isn't about luck—it's about strategy, creativity, and continuous refinement. By understanding your audience, telling compelling stories, leveraging data, and adapting to each platform's nuances, you'll set the stage for social media success. Remember: every post is an opportunity to connect, inspire, and grow. Start crafting your masterpiece today!

Learn the Secrets to Producing Engaging, Shareable, and Platform-Specific Content That Resonates with Your Audience

In today's fast-paced digital landscape, producing content that cuts through the noise is both a science and an art. With over 4.9 billion internet users as of 2023 and an average of 4.3 billion active social media users globally, the battle for attention has never been fiercer. If you want your brand or message to resonate, you need to craft content that's engaging, shareable, and tailored to specific platforms. Here's how to master this essential skill and thrive in the competitive world of digital media.

Step 1: Understand Your Audience

Content that resonates starts with a deep understanding of your target audience. Ask yourself:

Who are they? (Age, gender, location, interests, profession)

What do they value? (Education, humor, emotional connection, convenience)

Where do they consume content? (Instagram, LinkedIn, TikTok, YouTube, etc.)

Why do they share content? (To entertain, inform, inspire, or connect with others)

Real-World Example:

Consider Spotify's Wrapped campaign. By offering personalized insights into user listening habits, they transformed passive listeners into brand advocates. People shared their Wrapped stories over 60 million times in 2022 alone, proving the power of understanding and leveraging audience behavior.

Actionable Tip: Use analytics tools like Google Analytics, Facebook Insights, or TikTok's Creator Portal to identify key audience demographics and behaviors.

Step 2: Craft a Compelling Narrative

A good story is universal. Stories create emotional connections that facts and figures alone cannot. To craft a compelling narrative:

Start with a Hook: The first 3 seconds of your video or the opening line of your article must grab attention. Use bold claims, shocking statistics, or intriguing questions.

Build a Journey: Frame your content with a beginning, middle, and end. Highlight a problem, your solution, and the outcome.

Add Authenticity: Share real-life anecdotes or testimonials.

Data Insight:

According to HubSpot, 92% of consumers prefer ads that feel like a story. Content that features authentic storytelling has a 22x higher chance of being remembered than standalone facts.

Did You Know? The viral campaign "Share a Coke" by Coca-Cola personalized stories by replacing their logo with popular names, increasing consumption among young people by 7% in participating countries.

Step 3: Make It Shareable

People share content because it reflects their identity, beliefs, or aspirations. To make your content inherently shareable, focus on these pillars:

Emotion: Does your content make people laugh, cry, or feel inspired?

Utility: Is it helpful, insightful, or educational?

Relatability: Does it speak to shared experiences or values?

Example Breakdown:

Humor: Wendy's Twitter roasts have made the brand a cultural phenomenon. Their quick wit and relatable humor drive massive shares.

Emotion: Dove's "Real Beauty" campaign taps into empowerment and self-love, generating over 69 million views on YouTube.

Utility: Buzzfeed's listicles like "21 Easy Hacks for Everyday Life" provide actionable tips that users love to share.

Pro Tip: Create interactive elements like polls, quizzes, or templates. Canva's shareable templates are a prime example of how interactivity boosts virality.

Step 4: Tailor Content to Each Platform

Not all platforms are created equal. A one-size-fits-all approach rarely works. To maximize engagement:

Instagram:

Focus on high-quality visuals and concise captions.

Use hashtags and geotags to increase discoverability.

Leverage Stories, Reels, and carousels for varied content formats.

TikTok:

Create snappy, entertaining videos (7-15 seconds perform best).

Participate in trends and challenges.

Add captions and trending sounds for greater reach.

LinkedIn:

Share long-form, thought-leadership articles or industry insights.

Engage with professional discussions and network-building posts.

Include data-backed visuals like infographics.

Twitter:

Prioritize brevity (tweets with 71-100 characters get more engagement).

Jump into trending conversations with hashtags.

Post consistently during peak times for your audience.

Stat to Consider: Posts with videos see 48% more views on LinkedIn, while tweets with images get 150% more retweets.

Step 5: Leverage Analytics and Iteration

Once you've published your content, the work isn't over. Regularly analyze performance metrics and tweak your approach:

Engagement Rate: Are people liking, commenting, or sharing?

CTR (Click-Through Rate): Are they clicking on your links or calls to action?

Watch Time: Are viewers completing your videos?

Sentiment Analysis: What are people saying in the comments?

Optimization Techniques:

A/B Testing: Try different headlines, thumbnails, or CTAs to see what works best.

Repurposing: Turn a high-performing blog post into an infographic, video, or series of tweets.

Timing: Use tools like Sprout Social to identify the best posting times for your audience.

Insight: According to Social Media Examiner, businesses that analyze their metrics weekly see a 20% higher ROI from their social campaigns.

Strategic Content Trends for 2024

As the digital landscape evolves, staying ahead of trends is crucial:

Short-Form Video Dominance: Platforms like TikTok and Instagram Reels are shaping how content is consumed. 80% of internet users now prefer videos under 2 minutes.

AI-Generated Content: Tools like ChatGPT and Jasper.ai can enhance productivity but require human creativity for authenticity.

Social Commerce: Shoppable posts and live-streaming sales are bridging content and commerce.

Sustainability and Purpose-Driven Content: Gen Z and Millennials prioritize brands that align with their values.

Call to Action: Start experimenting with these trends now. Early adopters often reap the biggest rewards.

Producing engaging, shareable, and platform-specific content requires a mix of creativity, strategy, and data-driven decisions. Remember to:

Understand your audience deeply.

Tell stories that connect on an emotional level.

Design for shareability by tapping into humor, utility, and relatability.

Tailor your content to each platform's unique characteristics.

Analyze and iterate constantly.

Content that resonates doesn't happen by chance—it's the result of intentional effort and smart execution. By applying these principles, you can transform your content from forgettable to unforgettable, building stronger connections with your audience and achieving measurable results. So, what are you waiting for? Dive in and start creating content that truly makes an impact!

Chapter 3: The Power of Analytics and Metrics

Introduction: Numbers Tell a Story

Imagine throwing a party. You've spent weeks preparing, inviting people, setting up the decor, and planning the music playlist. But how would you know if your guests had a great time? Would you judge it by the smiles, the number of people dancing, or the leftovers on the table? The same principle applies to your social media efforts. Without analytics, you're hosting a blind party, unsure of what works and what doesn't.

Analytics and metrics are the pulse of your social media strategy. They're not just numbers; they're insights that reveal what captivates your audience, what content falls flat, and where your opportunities lie. In this chapter, we'll dive into why analytics matter, how to read them, and how to turn data into decisions that transform your online presence.

Why Analytics Matter: More Than Just Numbers

Clarity in Chaos: Social media can feel like a whirlwind. Posts, comments, likes, and shares happen so quickly that it's hard to keep track. Analytics provide clarity, offering a structured way to understand what's happening in your digital universe. For example, knowing that your Instagram Reels generate 60% more engagement than your static posts gives you the direction you need to create better content.

Measure Success: How do you know if your strategy is working? Numbers such as reach, engagement rate, and click-through rate (CTR) are indicators of success. For instance, a CTR of 4% might be stellar for one industry but average for another. Understanding these benchmarks helps you know where you stand.

Spot Opportunities: Data doesn't just tell you where you've been; it highlights where you could go. Maybe your Facebook audience is 70% women, but your product caters to men. That's a gap you can address with tailored campaigns.

Save Time and Money: Why waste resources guessing what your audience likes? Analytics let you focus on what's proven to work, cutting down trial-and-error efforts.

Key Metrics You Need to Know

Not all metrics are created equal. Let's explore the essential ones:

1. Reach and Impressions

Reach is the total number of unique users who saw your content.

Impressions count how often your content is displayed, whether clicked or not.

These metrics answer the question: *How far is my content spreading?* For example, a post with 10,000 impressions but only 2,000 reach means the same users are seeing it multiple times—a sign of strong recall.

2. Engagement Rate

This is the percentage of users who interact with your content (likes, comments, shares) compared to those who saw it.

Formula:

Engagement Rate = (Engagements / Reach) × 100

An engagement rate of 2% is average, while 6% or higher indicates highly engaging content. Consistent engagement signals a loyal audience.

3. Click-Through Rate (CTR)

CTR measures how many people clicked on a link in your post compared to how many saw it.

Formula:

CTR = (Clicks / Impressions) × 100

High CTR means your call-to-action (CTA) is compelling. If it's low, reconsider your wording or offer.

4. Conversion Rate

This tells you how many people completed a desired action, like signing up for a newsletter or purchasing a product, after clicking your link.

Formula:

Conversion Rate = (Conversions / Clicks) × 100

For e-commerce, even a 2% conversion rate can lead to significant revenue.

5. Audience Demographics

Understand who your audience is by analyzing data such as age, gender, location, and interests. For instance, discovering that 80% of your audience is aged 18-24 might influence a shift toward trendier, youth-focused content.

Tools to Simplify Analytics

If the thought of crunching numbers makes you uneasy, fear not. Today's tools make analytics user-friendly and actionable.

1. Platform-Built Tools

Instagram Insights: Provides data on reach, profile visits, and audience demographics.
Facebook Analytics: Tracks engagement, conversions, and ad performance.
Twitter Analytics: Shows tweet impressions, profile visits, and follower growth.

2. Third-Party Tools

Google Analytics: Perfect for tracking website traffic from social media campaigns.
Hootsuite Analytics: Offers in-depth reporting across multiple platforms.
Sprout Social: Visualizes data to help you understand trends and audience behavior.

3. Emerging AI Tools

Artificial intelligence tools like ChatGPT (yes, like me!) can interpret your data, suggest improvements, and even predict trends based on historical patterns.

Turning Insights into Action

Analytics without action are like a roadmap you never use. Here's how to transform insights into growth:

1. Identify Patterns

Look for recurring themes. Are posts with videos consistently performing better than text-based updates? Double down on what works.

2. Experiment and Optimize

Use A/B testing to compare different strategies. For example, try two headlines for a single post and see which garners more clicks.

3. Set SMART Goals

Use analytics to create Specific, Measurable, Achievable, Relevant, and Time-bound goals. Example: Increase Instagram engagement by 15% in three months by posting more Reels.

4. Monitor Competitors

Tools like SEMrush and BuzzSumo let you spy on competitors' top-performing content. This can inspire your own strategies.

5. Adjust Regularly

Social media trends evolve. Revisit your metrics monthly to ensure you're adapting to your audience's changing preferences.

Common Pitfalls and How to Avoid Them

Focusing on Vanity Metrics High follower counts look good, but they don't guarantee success. Engagement and conversion rates are more meaningful indicators.

Ignoring Negative Feedback Comments and messages criticizing your content or products can be goldmines for improvement. Addressing concerns boosts trust.

Overloading on Data Tracking too many metrics can overwhelm you. Stick to key performance indicators (KPIs) aligned with your goals.

Real-Life Success Story: Analytics in Action

Meet Maria, a small business owner who struggled to grow her candle company's online presence. After diving into her analytics, she discovered:

Her Instagram Reels had 3x the engagement of her static posts.

70% of her audience lived in colder regions where her winter-themed candles were popular.

Armed with this data, Maria focused her efforts on creating seasonal Reels and targeting cold-weather locations with paid ads. Within six months, her online sales doubled, and her Instagram followers grew by 40%.

Analytics are not just tools; they're your compass in the vast, ever-changing sea of social media. By understanding the numbers, you'll gain a deeper connection with your audience, unlock growth opportunities, and ultimately achieve success online. Remember, every metric is a stepping stone to mastery. So, embrace the power of analytics and let the data guide your journey.

Discover How to Measure Your Success, Optimize Your Strategies, and Use Data to Drive Better Decision-Making

Success in today's fast-paced world is no longer a matter of luck or vague intuition. It's about leveraging data, refining strategies, and making informed decisions to achieve measurable outcomes. Whether you're an entrepreneur, a team leader, or an aspiring professional, understanding how to track your progress and adapt your approaches is vital. In this comprehensive guide, we'll explore actionable insights and proven techniques for measuring success, optimizing strategies, and harnessing the power of data.

The Art and Science of Measuring Success

Success looks different for everyone. For some, it might mean reaching financial goals, while for others, it's about achieving personal growth or making an impact. Regardless of your definition, measurement is key to understanding progress.

Why Measure Success?

Measurement provides clarity. It tells you where you stand, how far you've come, and what's left to achieve. Research by McKinsey & Company shows that organizations with well-defined metrics are 20% more likely to exceed their goals. For individuals, a similar approach can lead to greater productivity and satisfaction.

Setting SMART Goals

The foundation of meaningful measurement lies in setting SMART goals:

Specific: Define what success means to you.

Measurable: Use numbers, timelines, or benchmarks to track progress.

Achievable: Set realistic goals based on available resources.

Relevant: Align your objectives with your broader purpose.

Time-bound: Establish deadlines to create urgency.

Example: Instead of saying, "I want to grow my business," opt for, "I aim to increase my monthly revenue by 25% within six months."

Key Performance Indicators (KPIs)

Identify metrics that align with your goals. For a marketer, KPIs could include website traffic, conversion rates, and customer retention. For a fitness enthusiast, it might be body fat percentage, strength gains, or race times. KPIs provide a clear snapshot of progress and areas for improvement.

Optimizing Your Strategies for Success

Once you've set goals and defined metrics, the next step is to optimize your strategies. This involves analyzing what works, experimenting with new approaches, and fine-tuning your methods.

Analyzing Your Current Performance

Start by reviewing your existing efforts. Gather data, whether it's sales reports, website analytics, or personal records. Tools like Google Analytics, Salesforce, or even a simple spreadsheet can help you identify trends and patterns.

Questions to ask:

Which strategies have yielded the best results?

What resources are underutilized?

Are there bottlenecks or inefficiencies?

Embracing Continuous Improvement

Optimization isn't a one-time activity. It's an ongoing process. Adopt a mindset of continuous improvement by:

Conducting A/B Testing: Test two versions of a strategy to see which performs better.

Gathering Feedback: Regularly ask clients, colleagues, or mentors for input.

Learning from Failures: Treat setbacks as learning opportunities.

Real-World Example: Amazon's relentless focus on customer feedback has enabled it to refine its services and dominate the e-commerce industry. Each adjustment—big or small—is rooted in data-driven insights.

Using Data to Drive Better Decision-Making

Data is the lifeblood of modern decision-making. It empowers you to act with confidence, minimize risks, and capitalize on opportunities. Here's how to make data your ally.

Collecting the Right Data

Not all data is created equal. Focus on data that aligns with your goals. If your objective is to improve customer satisfaction, track metrics like Net Promoter Score (NPS), response times, and feedback trends.

Data Sources:

Internal Data: Sales figures, employee performance, and customer feedback.

External Data: Market trends, competitor analysis, and industry benchmarks.

Real-Time Data: Social media analytics, live website traffic, and current stock levels.

Tools for Data Analysis

Leverage technology to simplify data collection and interpretation. Popular tools include:

Tableau: For advanced visualizations.

Excel: For customizable analysis.

Google Data Studio: For integrating multiple data sources.

Power BI: For enterprise-level insights.

Making Informed Decisions

Once you have the data, use it to inform your decisions. For example:

Strategic Decisions: Should you expand to a new market? Data on customer demographics and purchasing power can guide you.

Operational Decisions: How can you reduce costs? Analyze spending patterns and identify inefficiencies.

Personal Decisions: Should you invest in further education? Compare potential salary gains with the cost of tuition.

Real-Life Success Stories

Let's look at two examples of data-driven success:

Spotify's Personalized Playlists

Spotify uses user data to create personalized playlists like Discover Weekly. By analyzing listening habits, they've increased user engagement by 60%. This approach highlights the power of aligning strategies with user preferences.

Nike's Digital Transformation

Nike leverages data from its apps to understand customer behavior. Insights into workout habits and preferences have driven product innovation, resulting in a 40% increase in digital sales.

Tips for Staying Ahead

Stay Curious: The world of data is constantly evolving. Invest time in learning new tools and techniques.

Focus on Impact: Avoid getting lost in numbers. Concentrate on metrics that truly matter.

Act on Insights: Data is useless without action. Use your findings to implement meaningful changes.

Keep it Ethical: Always respect privacy and use data responsibly.

Measuring success, optimizing strategies, and making data-driven decisions are not just skills—they're competitive advantages. By adopting a systematic approach, you can unlock new levels of achievement and adapt to an ever-changing environment. Remember, the journey to success is iterative: set clear goals, measure progress, refine strategies, and use data to guide your way forward.

So, what's your next step? Start today. Define your goals, embrace the power of data, and take control of your success story. The tools and insights are within your reach—all you need is the commitment to act.

Chapter 4: Building Genuine Engagement and Community

Imagine this: You've spent hours crafting the perfect post—it's visually stunning, your caption is clever and concise, and your hashtags are on point. You hit "publish" with excitement, but hours later, the engagement is underwhelming. Likes trickle in, a comment or two appears, but the response isn't what you envisioned. Sound familiar? You're not alone. Millions of creators, brands, and entrepreneurs face this daily.

But here's the secret: thriving on social media isn't about chasing virality; it's about cultivating genuine engagement and building a community. Engagement isn't just about numbers—it's about connection. In this chapter, we'll explore the strategies to foster a loyal and active community, ensuring your efforts aren't lost in the vast ocean of content.

1. The Core of Engagement: Start with Value

Take a step back and ask yourself: Why should people engage with my content? This isn't rhetorical—it's the foundational question of every successful strategy. People engage with content that resonates, educates, entertains, or inspires. Your audience isn't there to serve you; you're there to serve them.

Action Plan:

Know Your Audience: Dive deep into analytics. Who are your followers? What do they like, dislike, need, or aspire to? For example, a fitness coach might notice their audience responds better to quick workout tips than long-form videos.

Deliver Solutions: If your niche is skincare, don't just post product selfies. Share advice like "5 Ways to Combat Dry Skin in Winter" or "The Science Behind Hyaluronic Acid."

Stat: According to a 2023 survey, 72% of users said they engaged most with content that provided direct value to their lives.

2. Engage Before You Post

This might sound counterintuitive, but some of the best engagement happens *before* your content even goes live. How? By engaging with others. Social media platforms reward users who actively interact with the community.

Action Plan:

Spend 15-30 minutes engaging with your audience before posting. Comment thoughtfully on their posts, reply to their stories, and like their content.

Interact with hashtags in your niche. For example, if you're a vegan chef, explore hashtags like #VeganRecipes or #PlantBasedLife and engage with relevant content.

Pro Tip: Your goal isn't to spam with generic comments like "Nice post!" but to leave thoughtful responses that spark conversation.

Stat: Instagram's algorithm prioritizes accounts that engage frequently, potentially boosting your post visibility by up to 25%.

3. Humanize Your Brand

People connect with people, not faceless brands. Even the biggest corporations have adopted a more relatable tone on social media. From Wendy's witty Twitter roasts to Duolingo's playful TikToks, authenticity and personality are key.

Action Plan:

Share behind-the-scenes moments. For example, show the messy desk where your creative ideas are born or the bloopers from your video shoots.

Use stories to talk directly to your audience. Treat them as if you were FaceTiming a friend.

Don't shy away from showing vulnerability. Did a product launch fail? Share what you learned. Did you hit a milestone? Celebrate with your followers.

Stat: A Sprout Social study found that 86% of consumers prefer an authentic and honest brand presence on social media.

4. Make Your Audience Feel Seen and Heard

Engagement is a two-way street. You can't expect your audience to engage with you if you don't reciprocate.

Action Plan:

Reply to Comments: This might seem basic, but many creators overlook it. A simple "Thank you!" or "Glad this resonated with you!" can go a long way.

Use Polls and Questions: Instagram's story features like polls, questions, and quizzes are engagement goldmines. For example, a travel blogger might ask, "Which destination should I visit next?"

Feature Your Followers: Repost user-generated content or shout out loyal followers. This not only strengthens connections but also encourages others to engage more.

Stat: Engagement rates increase by 30% when creators actively respond to comments and messages.

5. Consistency Over Perfection

Here's a truth bomb: consistency beats perfection every time. Your audience isn't looking for Hollywood-level production; they're looking for you. Consistency builds trust, and trust fosters community.

Action Plan:

Stick to a posting schedule. Whether it's three times a week or daily, be predictable.

Don't overthink. Sometimes, a simple post sharing a relatable moment or thought can outperform heavily curated content.

Pro Tip: Tools like Later, Buffer, or Hootsuite can help you schedule posts and maintain consistency.

Stat: Accounts that post consistently see a 33% higher engagement rate compared to sporadic posters.

6. Leverage Collaboration

Collaboration isn't just for influencers with millions of followers. Partnering with others in your niche can introduce you to a wider audience and foster genuine connections.

Action Plan:

Partner with creators or brands in your niche for giveaways, live sessions, or co-created content. For example, two fitness influencers could collaborate on a joint workout video.

Join and contribute to niche communities or groups, whether on Facebook, Reddit, or LinkedIn.

Stat: Collaborative posts on Instagram often see 2x the engagement compared to solo efforts.

7. Analyze, Adapt, and Evolve

Engagement isn't static. What works today might not work tomorrow. Successful creators are constantly analyzing their performance and adapting their strategies.

Action Plan:

Use platform analytics to track which types of posts perform best. Is your audience engaging more with videos, carousels, or single images?

Experiment with content formats and posting times. For example, if morning posts perform poorly, try evenings.

Stay updated with platform changes. Algorithms and features evolve; staying ahead of the curve gives you an edge.

Stat: Over 68% of successful creators revisit their content strategy quarterly.

8. Create a Culture of Community

Finally, remember that engagement isn't just about you—it's about them. Building a true community means fostering a sense of belonging among your audience.

Action Plan:

Encourage discussions among followers. For example, ask open-ended questions like, "What's the best advice you've ever received?" and actively moderate the responses.

Host virtual or in-person meetups. These events can deepen connections and strengthen loyalty.

Recognize and reward your community. Create exclusive perks for your most active followers, such as early access to content or discount codes.

Pro Tip: A Facebook group or Discord server can be a great way to centralize and nurture your community.

Stat: Communities where members feel valued report 80% higher engagement rates.

Building genuine engagement and community takes time, effort, and authenticity. There's no magic shortcut. But the rewards—a loyal audience, meaningful interactions, and sustainable growth—are worth every moment you invest.

Remember, your audience isn't just a metric. They're real people with thoughts, feelings, and dreams. Treat them as such, and you'll cultivate not just followers but advocates who champion your brand and mission.

So, what's your next step? Start today. Pick one strategy from this chapter, implement it, and watch your community grow. Because at the end of the day, social media isn't about algorithms; it's about connection.

Explore Proven Tactics to Foster Meaningful Interactions, Nurture Loyal Followers, and Turn Your Audience Into Advocates

Creating a loyal audience is not just about numbers; it's about meaningful connections that transform passive followers into active advocates. In this guide, we'll explore proven strategies to help you engage with your audience deeply, build loyalty, and inspire them to champion your cause.

1. Understanding Your Audience's Needs

Before you can create meaningful interactions, you need to understand your audience. Start by answering these questions:

Who are they? (Demographics, interests, and behaviors)

What challenges or desires drive them?

How can your brand provide value?

Actionable Tip: Use surveys, social media polls, and analytics tools to gather insights. For instance, a HubSpot study shows that businesses using buyer personas achieve a 73% higher conversion rate.

Engagement Example: A small eco-friendly fashion brand created a poll asking customers what sustainability topics they'd like to learn about. The result? A 150% increase in social media engagement the following week.

2. Fostering Two-Way Communication

Interacting with your audience should never feel one-sided. Encourage dialogue to build trust and mutual respect.

Proven Tactics:

Respond promptly: Aim to reply to comments or questions within 24 hours. Studies show that brands with fast response times on social media see a 48% higher likelihood of follower retention.

Host Q&A sessions: Live events on platforms like Instagram or Twitter Spaces provide real-time interaction.

Real-World Impact: Nike's social media team responds personally to customer inquiries. This strategy has significantly contributed to their 277M Instagram followers (as of 2023).

3. Delivering Value-Driven Content

People follow brands that educate, entertain, or inspire them. Regularly offer content that enriches their lives.

Ideas for Value-Driven Content:

How-to guides: Help solve their problems (e.g., a fitness app sharing beginner-friendly workout routines).

Exclusive insights: Share behind-the-scenes looks or upcoming trends.

Interactive posts: Quizzes, polls, or challenges increase engagement by up to 300%, according to Sprout Social.

Case Study: A vegan food blogger's weekly meal-prep videos led to a 40% growth in their YouTube subscribers in just 6 months.

4. Creating Loyalty Programs

Loyalty programs reward your audience for their continued support, turning followers into long-term advocates.

Effective Strategies:

Offer exclusive discounts or early access.

Create milestone rewards (e.g., celebrating a customer's 5th purchase).

Did You Know? According to Bond Brand Loyalty, 77% of consumers say loyalty programs make them more likely to stay with a brand.

Example: Starbucks' Rewards program contributed to a 7% increase in sales during the first year after its launch.

5. Building a Community Around Your Brand

Communities give your audience a sense of belonging, which is key to fostering advocacy.

Steps to Build a Thriving Community:

Create a dedicated space: Facebook Groups, Discord servers, or private forums.

Moderate discussions: Ensure the community feels safe and inclusive.

Encourage user-generated content: Highlight customer stories or testimonials.

Example: Peloton's Facebook Group boasts over 400,000 members who actively share workout tips and experiences. This sense of community fuels brand loyalty.

6. Empowering Your Audience to Advocate

Turning followers into advocates requires giving them tools to spread the word about your brand.

Simple Advocacy Strategies:

Referral programs: Dropbox's referral campaign increased signups by 60% in just one month.

Branded hashtags: Encourage followers to share their experiences (e.g., #ShareACoke).

Ambassador programs: Invite loyal followers to represent your brand.

Pro Tip: Recognize advocates publicly. A simple shoutout or feature can deepen their connection to your brand.

7. Consistently Measuring and Improving

Engagement strategies require ongoing refinement. Regularly analyze what's working and adapt.

Key Metrics to Track:

Engagement rate (likes, comments, shares)

Conversion rate (leads or sales from social media)

Advocacy rate (frequency of shares or recommendations)

Case Study: A software company that measured their Net Promoter Score (NPS) quarterly identified pain points and improved user satisfaction by 35% within a year.

People advocate for brands they genuinely trust and believe in. Building trust takes time, but with consistent effort and authentic interactions, you can foster a loyal audience that champions your brand for years to come.

Your Turn: Start small. Pick one tactic from this guide to implement this week and observe the results. Success lies in action—and you've got this!

Chapter 5: Monetizing Your Social Media Presence

Imagine waking up one day to realize that your passion for social media has turned into a thriving income stream. It's not just a fantasy; it's a reality for millions of individuals and businesses who've learned to monetize their online presence effectively. In this chapter, we'll uncover the proven strategies, tools, and mindsets that transform your social media from a pastime into a powerful revenue-generating machine.

Understanding the Value of Your Social Media Presence

Your social media accounts are more than just a digital scrapbook or promotional platform; they're assets. Whether you have 1,000 followers or 1 million, your audience represents potential customers, clients, and partners. According to Statista, the global influencer marketing industry reached $21.1 billion in 2023, a testament to the economic power of social media personalities.

Key Insight: Every follower represents more than just a number; they are a member of your community who trusts you to provide value, authenticity, and relevance. Leveraging this trust is at the heart of successful monetization.

Step 1: Choose the Right Monetization Model

There isn't a one-size-fits-all approach to earning money from social media. The best strategy depends on your niche, audience, and goals. Here are some common models to consider:

Sponsored Content: Brands are constantly looking for influencers to promote their products. If you've built a loyal and engaged audience, companies may pay you to create posts, videos, or stories featuring their offerings.

Example: A fitness influencer with 50,000 followers might charge $500–$1,000 per sponsored Instagram post.

Tip: Use platforms like AspireIQ, Upfluence, or CreatorIQ to connect with brands.

Affiliate Marketing: Earn a commission for every sale made through your unique affiliate links. This model works well for influencers in niches like fashion, tech, or health.

Example: A beauty YouTuber recommends a skincare product and earns 10% of every sale generated through their link.

Pro Tip: Promote products you genuinely love and use to maintain authenticity.

Selling Your Own Products or Services: Create and sell merchandise, digital products, or courses directly to your audience. This strategy allows you to retain full control over your revenue streams.

Example: A photographer sells Lightroom presets or online workshops.

Fact: According to Oberlo, eCommerce sales are projected to reach $6.3 trillion by 2024, showcasing the massive potential of direct sales.

Subscription-Based Models: Platforms like Patreon, Substack, and OnlyFans let you offer exclusive content for a subscription fee. This model works particularly well for creators who can provide niche content.

Case Study: A podcast host offers bonus episodes and behind-the-scenes insights for $5/month per subscriber.

Ad Revenue: Platforms like YouTube, TikTok, and Facebook allow creators to earn through ad placements in their content. While this requires meeting certain thresholds, it can become a steady income source.

Fact: YouTube pays creators 55% of the ad revenue their videos generate.

Step 2: Build and Nurture a Loyal Audience

Monetization starts with an engaged audience. A large follower count means nothing if your audience isn't interacting with your content. Prioritize quality over quantity by focusing on:

Consistency: Post regularly to keep your audience engaged.

Authenticity: Be genuine and relatable. Audiences can spot inauthenticity a mile away.

Engagement: Respond to comments, ask questions, and foster a sense of community.

Actionable Tip: Use analytics tools like Instagram Insights, YouTube Studio, or Google Analytics to understand what content resonates most with your audience.

Step 3: Establish Credibility and Authority

Brands and audiences alike are drawn to creators who exude trust and expertise. Showcase your authority by:

Sharing valuable insights or tips in your niche.

Collaborating with other respected creators.

Highlighting achievements or endorsements.

Real-World Example: When micro-influencer Sarah, a plant enthusiast, began sharing in-depth care guides and collaborating with a popular nursery, her follower count grew by 30%, and she landed a partnership worth $10,000.

Step 4: Diversify Your Income Streams

Relying on a single revenue stream can be risky. Explore multiple income sources to stabilize your earnings and maximize potential. For example:

Pair affiliate marketing with a subscription model.

Sell eBooks or courses while earning ad revenue.

Partner with brands but also promote your own merchandise.

Fact: A study by Influencer Marketing Hub found that top-earning influencers typically have 5-7 income streams.

Tools to Streamline Your Monetization Journey

Take advantage of technology to optimize your monetization strategy:

Canva: Create visually appealing posts and graphics.

Teespring: Design and sell merchandise with no upfront costs.

Kajabi: Build and sell online courses effortlessly.

Linktree: Consolidate all your links in one place for easy sharing.

Overcoming Challenges in Monetization

Monetizing your social media isn't without its challenges. Here's how to tackle common hurdles:

Burnout: Maintaining constant engagement can be exhausting. Avoid burnout by setting boundaries and scheduling content in advance.

Algorithm Changes: Stay informed about platform updates and diversify your presence across multiple platforms to reduce risk.

Rejection: Not every brand will want to collaborate, and that's okay. Focus on building your niche and delivering value.

Monetizing your social media presence is about more than just making money; it's about creating a sustainable ecosystem where your passion meets profitability. By understanding your audience, leveraging the right strategies, and staying authentic, you can unlock incredible opportunities.

Remember, every post, story, and interaction has the potential to pave the way for financial success. Start small, remain consistent, and watch your social media presence transform into a lucrative venture.

Challenge for You: Choose one monetization model discussed in this chapter and implement it within the next 30 days. Share your results with your audience and reflect on the journey. Success is closer than you think!

Uncover Strategies for Generating Revenue Through Ads, Partnerships, Product Sales, and Other Monetization Opportunities

Imagine this: you've built a platform, launched your dream product, or amassed a loyal audience. Now the question looms—how do you turn all that hard work into profit? Generating revenue isn't just about slapping ads on a website or relying on sporadic sales. It's about crafting a multi-dimensional strategy that maximizes every opportunity. In this guide, we'll dive into actionable strategies for ads, partnerships, product sales, and beyond. Buckle up, because by the end of this, you'll see monetization not as a challenge but as an exciting puzzle to solve.

1. Advertising: Monetizing Attention

Ads are one of the oldest monetization tricks in the book, but they've evolved far beyond basic banner ads. Here's how to maximize your revenue through advertising:

A. Programmatic Advertising

Leverage platforms like Google AdSense or Mediavine to display ads automatically tailored to your audience. Programmatic ads generated over **$418 billion globally in 2023**, and the numbers are climbing. The key? High traffic and a niche audience. If your blog, app, or site garners significant views, programmatic ads can offer consistent, passive income.

B. Native Advertising

Forget intrusive pop-ups; native ads blend seamlessly with your content. Platforms like Taboola and Outbrain allow you to embed ads that look and feel natural. For example, a fashion blog might feature sponsored articles showcasing trending styles—a strategy proven to boost engagement by up to **50%** compared to traditional ads.

C. Direct Sponsorships

As your platform grows, brands might approach you directly. This eliminates the middleman and gives you control over ad placement and pricing. For instance, YouTube creators with over **100,000 subscribers** can earn between $2,000 to $5,000 per sponsored video, depending on engagement metrics.

Pro Tip: Monitor ad performance with tools like Google Analytics or Hotjar. Analyze click-through rates (CTR) and adjust ad placements for maximum effectiveness.

2. Partnerships: Collaboration for Profit

Strategic partnerships can unlock revenue streams you hadn't even considered. From co-branded products to affiliate marketing, partnerships thrive on mutual benefit.

A. Affiliate Marketing

Promote a brand's product and earn a commission for every sale. Amazon's Affiliate Program is a classic example, offering up to **10% per sale**. Bloggers and influencers often earn six-figure incomes by aligning affiliate products with their niche.

Here's a case in point: A tech reviewer promoting gadgets through Amazon links. With **10,000 monthly visitors** and a conservative **1% conversion rate**, they could earn hundreds of dollars monthly—a small change that scales with traffic.

B. Co-Branded Campaigns

Partner with complementary businesses to create a win-win scenario. Consider this: a fitness influencer collaborates with a sports drink brand for a co-branded workout challenge. The influencer's audience engages with the challenge, while the brand gains exposure to a highly targeted audience. Such campaigns can yield ROI as high as **$5 for every $1 spent**.

C. Joint Product Launches

Take it up a notch by co-developing products with trusted partners. For example, a cooking influencer teaming up with a kitchenware brand to launch a signature line of cookware. This not only diversifies revenue but also strengthens brand credibility.

3. Product Sales: From Physical to Digital

Selling products is a classic revenue generator, but in today's digital-first world, the possibilities are boundless.

A. Physical Products

From custom merchandise to unique crafts, physical products remain a popular choice. Shopify reported that global e-commerce sales surpassed **$5.5 trillion in 2023**, proving the viability of online stores.

Key Steps to Succeed:

Find Your Niche: Sell what aligns with your brand. A fitness brand might sell gym equipment or supplements.

Dropshipping: Partner with suppliers to handle inventory and shipping. This model minimizes risk and upfront costs.

Market Effectively: Leverage social media ads or SEO strategies to drive traffic. Brands with effective digital marketing can see **3x ROI**.

B. Digital Products

Digital products have virtually no overhead. Think eBooks, courses, templates, or stock photography. Creators selling online courses, for instance, can earn upwards of **$50,000 annually**, depending on their niche and audience size.

Real-Life Example: A graphic designer selling customizable Canva templates priced at $20. With **500 sales monthly**, that's a $10,000/month revenue stream.

C. Subscription Models

Transform one-time buyers into loyal customers. Platforms like Patreon or Substack allow creators to offer exclusive content for a monthly fee. For example, a writer with 1,000 subscribers paying $5/month earns a steady $5,000 monthly income.

4. Diversified Monetization Opportunities

To truly unlock revenue potential, think beyond ads, partnerships, and product sales. Here are more strategies to consider:

A. Membership Communities

Create a premium community where members can access exclusive resources, networking opportunities, or mentorship. Fitness coaches, for example, can charge a monthly fee for access to workouts, meal plans, and direct interaction.

Stat Check: Communities with strong engagement boast retention rates exceeding **75%**, far outpacing typical subscription services.

B. Events and Workshops

Host live events or virtual workshops. A digital marketing guru could charge $500 per attendee for a day-long masterclass. With 50 attendees, that's $25,000 in revenue from a single event.

C. Licensing Content

Own intellectual property? License it to others. From stock images to educational resources, licensing ensures you earn revenue repeatedly from a single asset.

Fun Fact: Licensing contributed **$292 billion** to the global economy in 2023.

D. Monetize Expertise Through Consulting

Are you an authority in your field? Offer consulting services. Consultants can charge anywhere from $100 to $500 per hour, depending on their niche and experience.

5. Crafting a Holistic Revenue Strategy

Here's the secret sauce: Don't rely on a single monetization strategy. Diversify. For instance:

Use ads for consistent passive income.

Build affiliate partnerships for supplemental revenue.

Launch products (both physical and digital) for primary income streams.

Offer premium memberships to capitalize on loyal customers.

Test and Adapt

The digital landscape is dynamic. Test different strategies, analyze results, and refine. Use tools like A/B testing for campaigns or Google Analytics for traffic insights. Businesses that prioritize data-driven decisions see revenue growth rates **30% higher** than competitors.

Monetization isn't a one-size-fits-all approach. It's about understanding your audience, leveraging your strengths, and seizing opportunities. Whether it's ads, partnerships, product sales, or something entirely unique, the possibilities are endless. Remember: every great revenue stream started with a single bold step. So, what will yours be? Share your vision in the comments below, and let's turn dreams into dollars!

Appendices:

Appendix A: Social Media Toolkit

As a social media strategist, having the right tools at your disposal can make all the difference. Below is a curated list of tools, apps, and resources designed to streamline your workflow and maximize efficiency on social media platforms. Whether you're creating content, scheduling posts, analyzing performance, or engaging with your audience, these tools will help you stay ahead of the game.

1. Content Creation

Canva: Create eye-catching graphics, videos, and presentations with ease. Canva offers pre-designed templates for posts, stories, and ads across platforms.

Adobe Express: A simplified version of Adobe's design tools, ideal for creating polished content on the go.

CapCut: A versatile video editing tool that's perfect for creating engaging short-form content for TikTok and Instagram Reels.

2. Scheduling and Management

Hootsuite: Manage multiple accounts, schedule posts in advance, and track performance metrics all in one place.

Buffer: Known for its simplicity, Buffer allows you to plan and publish content seamlessly across platforms.

Later: Tailored for visual platforms like Instagram and Pinterest, Later's calendar view helps plan cohesive campaigns.

3. Analytics and Performance Tracking

Google Analytics: Understand traffic sources and how social media contributes to your website's performance.

Sprout Social: Combines publishing, monitoring, and analytics with in-depth reporting.

Social Blade: Tracks follower growth and engagement metrics, particularly for YouTube, Instagram, and TikTok.

4. Engagement and Community Management

Mention: Monitor brand mentions and engage with conversations around your brand or niche.

HubSpot's Social Inbox: Centralize social media conversations and respond quickly to your audience.

TweetDeck: An essential tool for Twitter power users to manage multiple streams and monitor trends in real time.

5. Collaboration and Workflow

Asana: Organize and track your social media projects with your team.

Trello: Visualize your workflow using boards, lists, and cards.

Slack: Keep your team aligned with real-time communication channels.

Pro Tip:

Experiment with free trials before committing to premium versions of these tools. Many offer insights into whether they're a good fit for your needs.

Appendix B: Platform-Specific Tips and Best Practices

Different platforms demand unique approaches to maximize impact. Here's a breakdown of actionable advice for each major social media platform.

Facebook

Content Type: Prioritize high-quality videos, infographics, and carousel posts.

Engagement Strategy: Utilize Facebook Groups to foster a sense of community and increase organic reach.

Timing: Post during late afternoons or evenings when most users are online.

Analytics Insight: Leverage Facebook Insights to track post reach, engagement, and demographics.

Instagram

Visuals First: Ensure your posts maintain a cohesive aesthetic and use high-resolution images.

Reels: Short, engaging videos perform exceptionally well. Use trending audio for greater visibility.

Hashtags: Research and use niche-specific hashtags for better discoverability.

Stories: Share behind-the-scenes content and leverage interactive stickers like polls and quizzes to boost engagement.

LinkedIn

Professional Tone: Focus on industry insights, thought leadership, and professional achievements.

Consistency: Post regularly and engage with comments to position yourself as an active contributor in your field.

Networking: Use LinkedIn's search tools to connect with industry peers, clients, or employers.

Articles: Publish long-form articles to demonstrate expertise and reach a broader audience.

TikTok

Trends Matter: Participate in challenges and use trending hashtags and sounds.

Authenticity Wins: Raw, unpolished content often resonates better than heavily produced videos.

Frequency: Post at least once daily to increase visibility.

Engagement: Reply to comments with video responses to deepen connections with your audience.

Twitter (now X)

Brevity is Key: Write concise tweets that pack a punch.

Visual Enhancements: Use images, GIFs, or short videos to capture attention.

Engagement: Participate in trending conversations and live-tweet during relevant events.

Threads: Share detailed insights or stories in threaded tweets for greater engagement.

Appendix C: Glossary of Social Media Terms

Navigating the social media landscape often involves a slew of industry-specific jargon. This glossary demystifies key terms to help you become fluent in the language of social media.

A

Algorithm: A set of rules used by social media platforms to determine what content is shown to users.

Analytics: Data insights used to measure the performance of your social media activities.

B

Boosting: Paying to promote a post to a larger audience.

Bounce Rate: The percentage of visitors who leave your site after viewing just one page.

C

Call-to-Action (CTA): A prompt encouraging users to take a specific action, such as "Sign up now" or "Learn more."

Click-Through Rate (CTR): The percentage of users who click on a link after seeing it.

E

Engagement: Interactions such as likes, comments, shares, and clicks on social media posts.

Evergreen Content: Content that remains relevant over time.

H

Hashtag: A keyword or phrase preceded by the # symbol used to categorize content.

Handle: A user's unique identifier on platforms like Twitter and Instagram (e.g., @username).

I

Impressions: The number of times your content is displayed, regardless of whether it was clicked.

Influencer: An individual with a significant following who can influence audience behavior.

K

Key Performance Indicator (KPI): A measurable value indicating the success of a social media strategy.

O

Organic Reach: The number of people who see your content without paid promotion.

Optimization: Adjusting content or strategies to improve performance.

S

Social Listening: Monitoring online conversations about your brand or industry.

Story: A short-lived post that disappears after 24 hours, available on platforms like Instagram and Facebook.

T

Trendjacking: Leveraging trending topics to increase visibility for your content.

Thread: A series of connected posts on platforms like Twitter.

U

User-Generated Content (UGC): Content created by users that features your brand or product.

URL Shortener: A tool that creates shorter links, such as Bitly, often used to track click metrics.

V

Viral: Content that rapidly gains popularity and is shared widely across the internet.

By utilizing the tools in Appendix A, adopting the platform-specific strategies in Appendix B, and mastering the terms in Appendix C, you'll be well-equipped to navigate and succeed in the dynamic world of social media. Remember, the key to mastery is staying informed, adapting to changes, and engaging authentically with your audience.

END

www.ingramcontent.com/pod-product-compliance
Lightning Source LLC
Chambersburg PA
CBHW030052230526
45471CB00003B/1065